THE WAY
OF THE
WISE

D0366163

THE WAY
OF THE
WISE

SIMPLE TRUTHS
for LIVING WELL

DR. KEVIN LEMAN

Revell

a division of Baker Publishing Group
Grand Rapids, Michigan

© 2013 by Dr. Kevin Leman

Published by Revell
a division of Baker Publishing Group
P.O. Box 6287, Grand Rapids, MI 49516-6287
www.revellbooks.com

Paperback edition published 2015
ISBN 978-0-8007-2242-5

Printed in the United States of America

The Library of Congress has cataloged the previous edition as follows:
Leman, Kevin.
    The way of the wise : simple truths for living well / Dr. Kevin Leman.
      p. cm.
    Includes bibliographical references.
    ISBN 978-0-8007-2157-2 (cloth) — ISBN 978-0-8007-2242-5 (ITPE)
    1. Bible. O.T. Proverbs III, 1–6—Criticism, interpretation, etc. I. Title.
BS1465.52.L46 2013
223′.706—dc23   2012029544

To protect the privacy of those who have shared their stories with the author, some details and names have been changed.

The internet addresses, email addresses, and phone numbers in this book are accurate at the time of publication. They are provided as a resource. Baker Publishing Group does not endorse them or vouch for their content or permanence.

To all who question God
and wonder where they fit in life's grid.
I think that covers just about all of us.

Do not forget my teaching,
  but keep my commands in your heart,
for they will prolong your life many years
  and bring you prosperity.
Let love and faithfulness never leave you;
  bind them around your neck,
  write them on the tablet of your heart.
Then you will win favor and a good name
  in the sight of God and man.
Trust in the LORD with all your heart
  and lean not on your own understanding;
in all your ways acknowledge him,
  and he will make your paths straight.

Proverbs 3:1–6

Contents

Contents

Acknowledgments

With appreciation to:

Two of the wisest women who have ever inhabited the planet: my mother, May Leman, and my wife, Sande.

My faithful editor, Ramona Cramer Tucker, who passionately takes the road less traveled.

Lonnie Hull DuPont, who always has my back, and Jessica English, for their stellar work on my behalf at Revell.

Introduction

Where Your Heart Is

I'm a guy who had little going for me early in life. Let's just say that Wisdom was not my middle name, and nobody on the planet would have called me wise.

Well, I take that back. Lots of people called me a wise guy. And a goofball and a comedian to boot. As a senior in high school, I was in consumer math, where the final exam question was something like this: "Jane went to the store to buy tangelos. She had a dollar and came home with four tangelos. How much did each tangelo cost?"

The funny (or sad) part is, I never reached that final exam in the course because I literally chased the teacher out of the classroom with my antics. The school kicked me out of the class after the teacher resigned and got a sub to finish the rest of the year. On my high school transcript, there's no grade for consumer math—only a hyphen.

I didn't want any part of those I saw as representatives of Christianity. I thought they were weird, strange, and . . . well, those descriptions would be kind.

When I applied to over 160 colleges, nobody wanted me. Finally, through a series of events, I got admitted to North Park University in Chicago. (Actually, I think they'd prefer to remain anonymous; nevertheless, they finally let me in through some miracle.) But long story short, I was asked to move along in the first quarter of my sophomore year.

So I came to Arizona at 19 years old and got a job. Of course, I wanted an executive-level position that paid a lot of money, but the only offer I received was a janitor job at a local hospital.

At that point in my life I had no use for God. Did I believe in him? Sure. He was the almighty guy "up there." But he didn't have any connection to my life. And I didn't want any part of those I saw as representatives of Christianity. I thought they were weird, strange, and

... well, those descriptions would be kind. Christians turned me off in more ways than you can imagine.

But God does move in mysterious ways. And behind God, many times there is a person. That person was my mom, who wrote in my Bible the words of Proverbs 3:1–6. They lingered there until at last I opened that Bible and was ready to consider the words seriously.

When I first read Proverbs 3:1–6, I thought, *Wow, anyone who follows these little nuggets can't go wrong.* The instructions seemed so simple, so straightforward, that even a guy like me could follow them.

But then, as I pondered the words more, I was awestruck. These words, I realized, were the road map to a win-win life. King Solomon brilliantly finagled 10 of life's most practical and meaningful principles into 6 tight little verses. No wonder he became the wisest king to rule Israel in long-ago times. Even more, if you understand and take these verses to heart and they become a part of your life and belief system, I'm convinced you'll leave an astounding legacy that will influence generations to come.

That's why this compact book is crafted to jump-start or revitalize your spiritual life by unlocking the secrets of those 10 powerful principles. It'll give you hope, courage, inspiration, a fresh perspective, and some humor along the way—all in an easily readable package. (If you want to read a long book, I'd suggest James Michener's *Hawaii*. I recently saw a man on a long flight attempting to read it. When I asked him if he thought he'd ever finish it, he grinned and said, "Of course not. But my wife wanted me to try.")

Proverbs 3:1–6 has everything to do with who you are, where your heart is, who you think God is, and who you want to become.

1

Words That Pack a Wallop

Do not forget my **teaching**.

<small>PROVERBS 3:1A</small>

I believe highly in teachable moments. I've been talking to parents about teachable moments for years. But sometimes we're bombarded with so much information that we forget to remember what's truly important in life. The words of Proverbs 3:1–6 pack a powerful punch if we keep them in mind.

But to accept teaching, you have to be a student who is open to being taught.

When I was a kid, I wasn't teachable. I didn't do well in school. Maybe part of that is because I cut classes every time I could. My saintly mom was in school, talking to the principal, more than I was in class. I had the life philosophy that I only counted when I got others' attention. I was good at making people laugh and have a fun time. And when I succeeded at that, I was one happy dude.

The first teachable moment I can remember is when a teacher said to me in April of my senior year, "Leman, did you ever think you can use the skills you have to do something positive?" That was an eye-opener for me— the first time someone actually said I had any skills.

And another light went on the month the high school seniors started announcing where they were going to college. I said to myself, *You know what? You're an absolute fool. Wasting your time. People enjoy your antics, but you're going to be left behind.*

So I decided I'd better go somewhere for college too. After wrangling my way with begging, I eked out a C-minus average the first year of college. That should have been proof to me that there was a living God and that he had a plan for my life. Especially since Cs in those days were earned Cs, not the easy-B mentality some educators have today.

But my reign at college didn't last. In my sophomore year, I was asked not to come back.

God had more teachable moments in mind for me. My parents had moved to Tucson, Arizona, so I followed them there and got the high-class job I'd always longed for . . . as a janitor at a local hospital.

For the first time in my life, I realized intensely what it felt like to be treated as a second-class citizen. At first I worked in the main building and wore a steel-gray janitor's uniform. Then I moved up to mopping the floor in labor and delivery.

It was amazing the transformation in people's attitudes toward me. I wore

I eked out a C-minus average the first year of college. That should have been proof to me that there was a living God.

surgical greens, had a mask, and wore a cap. When I had them on, I was somebody. There were even times when people would mistake me as a doctor and address me as "Doctor" or "Sir"—even if I looked awfully young for a resident or intern. At home, I made a little sign with one of those label makers and attached the strip to my bedroom door:

KEVIN: FLOOR SURGEON

Those were difficult days because I wasn't going anywhere, and I'd started to realize that. In hindsight, though, God was providing teachable moments that would serve me well in the future. I discovered I had the ability to make being a janitor sort of a fun thing. And I learned how to save money and spend it wisely.

> *I was busily mopping the men's room when the prettiest young woman I've ever laid eyes on . . . came in to help a little old guy go potty.*

I also had no idea at that time that getting a job as a full-time janitor, making $195 a month, would lead me to the one person whom God would use to get my life in order . . . and that I'd meet her in the men's room. You've got to admit that's a little far-out, but I've learned that with God, all things are possible.

Long story short, I was busily mopping the men's room when the prettiest young woman I've ever laid eyes on—I'm talking *gorgeous*—came in to help a little old guy go potty. Well, I was good at saying stupid things, and what I said next was a real class act. When Sande's and my eyes met that day, I said, "Would you like to go to the World's Fair with me?"

No kidding. That's the first thing I said to the woman who is now my wife. Note that the World's Fair was in New York, and we were in Tucson, Arizona. And on a salary of $195 a month, two first-class tickets to New York weren't possible.

Sande, to her credit, simply said, "Well, I don't know."

So I moved quickly to "How about lunch then?"

Boy, was I ever stupid.

We shared a 20-cent cheeseburger. (Now, if you can remember the 20-cent cheeseburger and the 15-cent hamburger at McDonald's, you're going to die soon. Needless to say, it was a long time ago.) We also split a 10-cent Coke. I was always a big spender. Thirty cents plus tax. And taxes then sure weren't what taxes are today. But I digress.

I fell like a ton of bricks in love with this woman. When Sande met me, I was one handsome dude in my steel-gray janitor's uniform. On the sleeve near the shoulder there was a patch that read "Tucson Medical

Center" in an inverted U shape, and it had "Housekeeping" on the bottom of it with the image of a crossed broom and mop. Talk about a great self-image for a 19-year-old kid. Even more, I had a capped front tooth that had worn through, so my tooth looked like it had a big dark spot in the middle of it. I'm tellin' you, I was a real stud.

> *The head nurse pulled her aside in a matronly way one day to tell her, "Don't associate with that janitor. He'll never amount to anything."*

To this day, people meet Sande, my looker wife, and give her the fish eye, then look over at me, her chubby husband. I can see what they're thinking—especially the men, who don't hide their thoughts well: *Holy cow, how did THAT happen?*

There's a great country western classic called "She Believes in Me" by Kenny Rogers. And that's what Sande—Mrs. Uppington, as I lovingly call her sometimes because she's such a classy lady—did. She believed in me . . . even when we were dating and the head nurse pulled her aside in a matronly way one day to tell her, "Don't associate with that janitor. He'll never amount to anything."

Those were words that packed a wallop—words that would drive a baby of the family like me toward success. And they worked.

I was a punk. I dressed like a punk. I smoked Salem cigarettes. I was a screwball. But I was beginning to understand life's teachable moments. I was learning that things had to be done differently in my life. The teaching began with my mom and expanded through Sande—both "ordinary" women whose beliefs and words were used to do extraordinary things in my life.

Her words packed a powerful punch because she lived out her beliefs in front of me.

Sande didn't beat me over the head with her "religion." I loved her enough that I chose to go to church with her. She didn't say, "It's disgusting to kiss you because you smell like an ashtray, and you taste like one too." That incredible woman used great restraint . . . and prayed . . . and continued to believe in me.

Her words packed a powerful punch because she lived out her beliefs in front of me.

I always ask people when I'm speaking, "Who believed in you?" And then I say, "If you're a success in life in any area, it's because perhaps one person believed in you. If you had two people who believed in you, you're really blessed."

Others' belief in you starts off your spiritual pilgrimage . . . even if you don't know you're on one, as I didn't.

Jump ahead a few years in my life to see what a difference my mom's and Sande's belief in me made. After I got all my academic degrees, I became a professor at the University of Arizona. I taught open forum counseling. In other words, my classroom was not merely a class of theory and academics, it was applied psychology in action—a very unusual class in its day. I'd bring in a real family struggling with their marriage or their kids, and I would counsel them in an open forum area. I literally taught my students how to counsel by walking them through the process. I'd go ahead and counsel the family, then I'd step out of that counseling role and face the students.

"Now let me tell you what I just did and why and explain what's really going on in this family," I'd say.

People were on the edge of their seats. I never had a problem with my students being bored or falling asleep, because the class was action-packed and tremendously popular.

That's what King Solomon did in Proverbs 3:1–6. He brilliantly figured out that to make the maximum impact, his words had to be action-packed. They had to clearly show anyone who read them what to do—in a very compact way that any person could understand.

"Do not forget my teaching," he said. Clear-cut. Simple. And life-transforming.

I knew all the Sunday school stories— my mom had dragged me to church every week. I thought the teaching was going in one ear and out the other. I chose not to follow it. But because of my mom's gentle persistence, I came back to the teaching I thought I'd forgotten. And it truly transformed my life.

I knew all the Sunday school stories—my mom had dragged me to church every week.

You see, God can do a work in your life even when you don't know it.

That's why I love the old poem "Footprints in the Sand." The poet asks God why, during the roughest times of life, she can see only one set of footprints in the sand. Does that mean God left her?

God's reply? "Hey, those are the times when I was carrying you. You were never alone!" When I look back on all aspects of my life, there is no doubt: God had his hand on me long before I knew who he was. I could never forget his teaching, because his teachable moments followed me all along the way . . . and carried me in my darkest moments.

They will carry you too.

Things to Ponder . . .

"Do not forget my teaching."
PROVERBS 3:1A

Who believed in you? Write a note to that person and say, "Thank you for making a difference in my life." Everyone can use a little encouragement.

What have you done to provide teachable moments for those you love? To express your belief in them?

If Almighty God is in your corner, there's nothing to fear.

2

"Jesus and God, Jesus and God, That's All They Talk about— Jesus and God"

Keep my commands in **your heart**.

PROVERBS 3:1B

I love Chuck Swindoll. I've always been sort of a groupie of his. One day when I was listening to his radio show, I heard him tell a great story about his visit to a young children's Sunday school class. It went something like this:

"What's green and says 'ribbit'?" he asked the children.

A little boy frowned and appeared thoughtful. "Well," he said slowly, "I think it's a frog, but I'll say Jesus."

Chuck was puzzled. "Why would you say that?"

"Because we're in Sunday school," the little boy said, "and that's all we ever talk about here—Jesus and God."

Another mom told me the story about her young boy muttering something as he sat in the backseat of the car on the way home from church. After listening carefully, she finally got the gist of it: "Jesus and God, Jesus and God, that's all they talk about—Jesus and God."

Out of the mouths of babes always comes wisdom. Could it be that, in the push to sound "spiritual" or be "Christlike," we actually miss the heart of the matter about who Jesus and God really are?

If you ask people to point to themselves, guess where they'll always point.

To their head?

No.

To their feet?

No.

They'll point right to their heart. That's because the heart is the center of a person.

The heart informs the way you respond and react, the way you treat others, and the way you view yourself and God. You can sound spiritual, be able to recite the Ten Commandments, know the Four Spiritual Laws *ad nauseam*, and appear successful in every arena of life, but if your heart isn't focused on the big picture of what really matters, all the words you say won't mean squat. You won't treat others the way that God would want you to treat them. You won't love as Christ commands you to love.

Could it be that, in the push to sound "spiritual" or be "Christlike," we actually miss the heart of the matter about who Jesus and God really are?

As a guy who gets more than his fair share of Pharisee-like letters and emails from folks who don't like something I write or say in a seminar, I can tell you on a personal level it never feels good to be criticized. But if I'm really going to respond the way I need to—as God would have me respond—I need to take the advice of my dear wife.

One day after I'd read a letter to Sande where someone majorly ripped into something I'd said at an event, she said, "Leemie, it's easy to love those people who think you're wonderful. It's difficult to love those people who think you're a real jerk."

> "It's easy to love those people who think you're wonderful. It's difficult to love those people who think you're a real jerk."

Take, for instance, what Jesus said: "When someone slaps you, turn the other cheek toward them and let 'em have a go at the other side" (Leman translation).[1] You might be thinking, *Why on earth would I do that?* Because when Jesus walked on this earth, he showed love at all costs.

But did he let people walk all over him? Certainly not. When he saw the money changers in the temple—the house of God—making their profits, did he say, "Oh, hi, fellas! Have a nice day"?

Far from it. He overturned the tables in a fiery wrath that crashed them all to the floor and drove those people right out of the temple.

What can we learn from Jesus about dealing with tough situations and difficult people? Sometimes you should turn the other cheek. Other times you need to take a firm stand. You overturn the tables. You take action. God has given each of us a brain, and discretion is part of living the Christian life.

So back to my anger over the letter I received and Sande's response. She went on to tell me, "I know that letter doesn't sound good, and it hurts your feelings and makes you angry. It completely misperceives your heart on that matter. Nevertheless, you've got to love *everyone*, not just those who agree with you. That's the measure of living a Christian life."

You see why I married that woman? Mrs. Uppington is so smart . . . and she's *nearly* always right. This baby of the family needs her calm, logical common sense.

When someone offends you, it's much easier to blow them off—or punch them out (of course, in a Christian, loving way). The more difficult thing is to listen and love *in spite of others' actions*. And also to discern that moment when you need to overturn the tables and take action yourself.

Jesus was always loving toward children and those in deep pain. But he was also one big pain in the keister for the Pharisees—the self-righteous ones who were all about the law but were really like whitewashed tombs on the inside. He presented so many problems for them that they were constantly badgering him and trying to back him into a corner with their fancy rhetoric.

Jesus never fell for their schemes. He bluntly nailed them by saying exactly the right thing. You see, he discerned the motives behind their questions.

But sometimes your head will tell you one thing and your heart another. The epiphany comes when you take the information you know and transfer it from your head to your heart. You can say all the right things, but if you don't live out what you believe, you're an empty aluminum can clanging down the street.

So let me ask you. What do you think about God? Is there really a God? Does he really exist? And if so, how can you get your mind around the concept of such a God? In what ways will the things you learn about him change what you do and say on a daily basis?

I'm convinced we need to think our way to our heart. What do I mean by that?

As an author, I've often picked up books by various other authors that are filled cover to cover with deep, theological thoughts. I never did understand the majority of them. They were a little too deep for me. I knew there was a message in there somewhere, but I guess I was one of those few on the planet who wasn't smart enough to figure it out.

To me, believing in God or not believing in God is a little simpler.

I'm talking about the fact that you can believe that some amino acids got together in space billions and billions of years ago. And from those amino acid collisions came all the astounding varieties of hyacinths, daffodils, frogs, centipedes, elephants, dinosaurs, and human beings.

If you believe that, you've got a lot of faith. More than I do. In fact, I'll give you an A for effort on that one.

If you don't believe God is the Creator, take a look at Psalm 22:

> My God, my God, why have you forsaken me?
>   Why are you so far from saving me,
>   so far from the words of my groaning? . . .
>   A band of evil men has encircled me,
>   they have pierced my hands and my feet. . .
> They divide my garments among them
>   and cast lots for my clothing.[2]

Now flash forward to the book of John.

> This happened that the scripture might be fulfilled which said, "They divided my garments among them and cast lots for my clothing." So this is what the soldiers did.[3]

Psalm 22 was written by David a thousand years before Christ, yet it contains some of Christ's exact words on the cross. How can that not be God? Could *you* predict word for word what someone would be saying or feeling a thousand years from now? Even more, those words and actions are recorded in not only *one* of the four Gospels of his life but *all four*.[4]

Then add to that the fact that Jesus' birth was prophesied 700 years before he was born. Even more, multiple prophesies that Old Testament writers predicted would happen actually happened exactly as they said.[5]

Take this one, for example:

> He was pierced for our transgressions,
>   he was crushed for our iniquities;
> the punishment that brought us peace was
>   upon him,
>   and by his wounds we are healed.[6]

Then do your own comparison with how Matthew, Mark, Luke, and John spoke of his crucifixion 700 years later! Amazing. Mind-boggling.

Maybe I'm simpleminded, but proof like that makes me say, "Shazam! This God is who he says he is."

When I examine this evidence and let the truth of it flow from my mind into my heart, I realize I shouldn't be so cavalier toward God, so lukewarm in my appreciation of who God is. I ought to be awestruck by his majesty, power, greatness, and holiness.

Instead, some of us have reduced God to a $25 bottle of miracle water from televangelist Billy Bob . . . or reduced Jesus to a "friend and buddy" who listens to our bedtime prayers.

You can say all the right things and do all the right things, but if you don't live out what you believe, you're an empty aluminum can clanging down the street.

Why *should* we talk about Jesus and God? Because there is no one else like them, and there never will be. They are completely, utterly unique.

Even more, God knows us through and through. He knows how imperfect and weak and doubting we are as human beings. That's why, after his resurrection, he appeared to so many people. He could have done it only once—announced himself to the women, who he knew would spread the word—then disappeared forever. Instead he showed up multiple times, including to his disciples as they were in hiding.

> *God knows us through and through. He knows how imperfect and weak and doubting we are as human beings.*

Picture the disciples with me at that moment. They were all huddled together behind locked doors, jumping at the least little sound, and scared to death. They were fearful that since they'd been seen with Jesus, somebody was going to crucify or lynch them. Then guess who appeared miraculously in their midst? Never mind the locked door. It was Jesus himself. God in the flesh! We're talking supernatural here, because there's no other way it could have happened.

I'm sure the disciples trembled. A few might even have had to check their pants. (I know I would.) They were shocked. At first they disbelieved their eyes. *That can't be Jesus standing there. He's dead.*

Then a few of them started to get it. *But you know, he said he'd rise again. . . .*

Then, all of a sudden, their disbelief and fear flamed to pure elation and belief. A faith so strong that they'd never back down again—even under great persecution.

Why did Jesus show himself to so many different people in so many different situations? Because he knew how hard it would be for some to believe.

A lot of people find themselves in that position today. They find it hard to believe. Maybe you do too.

> *Why did Jesus show himself to so many different people in so many different situations? Because he knew how hard it would be for some to believe.*

When Jesus walked on this earth, he loved to connect with people, and they wanted to connect with him. They wanted to touch his garment. To touch him. They believed that simply touching Jesus would cure their illnesses and change their lives.

Today God has left his touch—his fingerprints—all over his creation. And I'm completely in awe. Basking in the loveliness of the flowers and mountains that surround my home in Arizona solidifies my faith. If you're searching for proof that God exists, take a look around. Gaze at a sunset, admire a stalk of Queen Anne's lace, dangle your feet in a stream, or stare into the eyes of a four-year-old. Somehow that theory of amino acids colliding and reorganizing themselves doesn't seem very real anymore, does it?

This earth is suspended in thin air and hung at exactly the right degree. Physicists tell us that if it was just one degree one way, we'd freeze. One degree the other way, and we'd fry.

No matter what even the smartest of scientists say, they can't look at the whole picture without having some measure of faith. The problem is, so many of them (and we regular human beings too) don't want to believe, because doing so would require a heart response. And that would mean changing some part of their life they don't want to change.

But the evidence of our intricate universe loudly proclaims the truth of how perfectly attuned God's creation is. For example, this earth is suspended in thin air and hung at exactly the right degree. Physicists tell us that if it was just one degree one way, we'd freeze. One degree the other way, and we'd fry.

That same God cared so much about the intricacies of the earth and beauty that he created the flowers of the field (in such brilliant profusion and variety) and the birds and mammals of the earth (including pelicans, storks, penguins, and anteaters). The creation surrounding us every day shows us that God is personal . . . and that he has a sense of humor too.

God has always existed. He has no beginning, no end. No one created God.

Now there's another mind-boggling thought, especially since everything we see on earth has a beginning, and everything we experience in life has an end. God indeed knows the measure of our lives from their very beginning to their very end. He knows our life purpose.

> Before I formed you in the womb I knew you,
> before you were born I set you apart.[7]

But it's one thing to have head knowledge (to know about God and be able to spout off a Bible verse); it's another to experience the mystery, miracle, and awesomeness of God's power at work in the universe—and in you.

Remember the two little boys at the beginning of the chapter—the one who knew a frog was green and said "ribbit" but thought he better say "Jesus" since it was Sunday school, and the one in the backseat who said, "Jesus and God, Jesus and God, that's all they talk about—Jesus and God"? There is a lot of wisdom in those statements?

But for both those boys, there was a disconnect. No one connected the dots for them between people talking about Jesus and God and who Jesus and God really are. You can't just *believe* in Jesus and God. You have to connect the dots from believing with your head to having a personal relationship with Jesus and God—the kind of relationship that becomes integral to who you are, what you do, and how you act.

To incorporate who Jesus and God really are, you have to not only know *about* them but *know them personally*, and then incorporate that knowledge into your heart, where it can take up residence. For that's when true transformation happens—when you get your heart involved in the matter.

Things to Ponder . . .

"Keep my commands in your heart."

PROVERBS 3:1B

What commands give you the most difficulty? What is in your heart that makes it hard for you to follow those commands?

How can you move this week from knowing *about* God to *knowing him personally*?

Moving takes conscious effort and heartfelt commitment.

3

Jesus Ain't the Big, Bad Wolf

For they will **prolong your life** many years.

PROVERBS 3:2A

Remember the classic childhood story "The Three Little Pigs"? Before the three innocent little darlings go off into the world, Mama Pig gives them sage advice: "Whatever you do, do it the best that you can because that's the way to get along in the world."[1]

The first little pig builds his house out of straw because it's the easiest thing to do. Before noon, he's napping in the shade of a nearby tree, sipping a piña colada.

The second little pig builds his house out of sticks. He's satisfied he's got a stronger house than his brother.

The third little porker builds his house out of bricks, because he's determined to craft a house that will withstand anything.

When the big, bad wolf sees his new neighbors, he knows he's got it made. Dinner à la carte without even breaking a sweat. He goes to the little pig in the house of straw first.

"Let me in," he orders, "or I'll huff, and I'll puff, and I'll blow your house in."

"Not by the hair of my chinny chin chin," the fat little pig says.

But of course he gets eaten anyway.

Ditto with pig two, in the house of sticks, the very next evening. The big, bad wolf is dining high on the hog.

The third night, the wolf tries the same scare tactics with the third little porker holed up in his house of bricks. "Let me in, or I'll huff, and I'll puff, and I'll blow your house in!" he growls.

But the third pig is smarter than his two other siblings. He knows his house will hold up, so he simply goes about the business of making his own dinner.

The big, bad wolf cleverly climbs on the roof, looking for a way down.

But the pig is more clever yet. He puts a pot of water to boil in his fireplace. When the big, bad wolf comes down the chimney, where does he end up? Right in the pig's boiling pot. And that was the end of the big, bad wolf.

Indeed, that pig learned well from his mama to go about life the very best way he could. The first two pigs had a short and very stressful life span, since they didn't learn their lesson very well.

But back up to the big, bad wolf for a moment. Isn't that the way some of us think of God? As the big, bad wolf in the sky who is going to huff and puff and blow our house in? The judgmental guy who's ready to hammer us for the least infraction of the rules? Who never wants us to have any fun? Who is always stacking the odds *against* us and is never *for* us?

> "Let me in, or I'll huff, and I'll puff, and I'll blow your house in!"

Did you ever think that the way you view God has everything to do with the way you live your life, including the kind of stress you live under?

"I'm so stressed out."

If you gave me a dollar for the number of times I've heard that phrase (or the hundreds of variations of it) in the last year, I'd have more money than someone who wins the million-dollar lottery (and then has to pay over 38 percent of it in taxes).

"I'm so stressed out."

Stress is the name of the game for everyone from business executives to stay-at-home moms to junior high athletes. In "Effects of Stress," wellness expert Elisabeth Kuhn says:

> Excessive, untreated stress can actually kill you. When you're stressed, your body produces the hormone cortisol, which is designed to get your rear in gear as part of the fight-or-flight mechanism. However, this hormone is meant to be released only occasionally in small doses—when stress causes it to be secreted for long periods of time, the body reacts with a variety of different health consequences.[2]

Stress is such an integral part of life that I wrote an entire book on the subject: *Stopping Stress before It Stops You*. But where is this stress coming from?

Could it be that we're trying too hard to control our life circumstances? That we're doing too much because we're not comfortable with who we are and are striving to be someone we're not? Might we be creating stress by our poor choices—and our driving need to be in charge?

There are some who strongly believe we can become so addicted to adrenaline—the kind our body produces due to busy schedules—that we want and need to stay on the conveyor belt of life.

But when we focus first on God's teachings, they help us cut through the clutter of our busyness to what we really need to do. They help us prioritize so we can let some things go and live life the way God has intended us to live—with our head and our heart unified on what is most important. And doing so actually gives us a healthier life, lengthening our life span. Numerous studies show that people who are faithful in marriage and have positive attitudes—and therefore have less stress—live much longer lives.[3]

> *We can become so addicted to adrenaline . . . that we want and need to stay on the conveyor belt of life.*

When I surveyed women, asking them, "What are the major stressors in your life? List them in order," the responses were clear. Without a doubt, the top six stressors for women are children, lack of time with loved ones, husbands, household chores, finances, and work. Now isn't it like women to put relationships first? (Survey men and you'll get a different response, with relationships often in the backseat.)

Stress is a fact of life. It's what we do with it that either makes or breaks us.

Take John, a guy who was in a blue-collar job he didn't really like but kept doing it to make ends meet. Problem was, he spent too much of his income in bars. He was an okay guy when sober, but look out if he'd had a few too many brewskis. Then he would take out his frustration on his family and do irrational things that caused all of them stress.

For example, one night his friends brought him home from a drinking binge. The next day he couldn't remember where he'd left the family car.

Another night, when he'd had too much to drink, his wife decided to stay overnight at their son's house. John was the old-fashioned sort, so he phoned his son and demanded that his wife come home immediately. "A woman needs to be with her husband," he insisted.

The son said calmly, "It sounds like you've had too many beers. Mom will stay with us tonight. You sleep it off and we'll see you in the morning."

So John, in a froth, got in the car and drove to his son's house. When he missed the driveway and tried to turn around, his car got stuck on a boulder. He spun the wheels and blew out the tires.

> *Stress is a fact of life. It's what we do with it that either makes or breaks us.*

Furious and tipsy, he tried to get out of the car . . . and fell on a prickly pear cactus. Someone saw him and called 9-1-1. By 3:30 a.m., he was in the hospital, getting prickly pear needles pulled one by one out of his you-know-what.

You'd think having such a pain in the keister would make a pain-in-the-keister guy turn his life around.

But some folks simply don't learn. I call it *developmental carnality*. I love that term. The older I get, the more I realize that my carnal self is never far behind me. That's why people who come across as righteous, but are far from it when you peel away the wrappings, make me sorta sick. Jesus couldn't stand the Pharisees and continually gave them the what for. He called it like he saw it: "You whitewashed sepulchers!"[4]

> *Jesus couldn't stand the Pharisees and continually gave them the what for. He called it like he saw it.*

But he had all sorts of wonderful things to say about people like the widow, who only had a tiny, tiny mite (think of it as less than a penny), yet she gave it with a heart full of joy for the blessings God had given her. She gave even when she wasn't sure if she'd have anything for supper.

And Jesus always encouraged children to come to him, calling to attention the simplicity and beauty of childlike faith.

When my five-year-old granddaughter lost her first tooth and I was tucking her in bed that night, she asked me, "Grandpa, what does the tooth fairy look like?"

I smiled. "She looks like Tinkerbell."

If only we could all maintain the faith of a little child to believe in miracles and things that don't make sense and therefore require that leap of faith.

But as we grow older, we lose our childlike innocence as life and troubles creep in. It's like attaching an IV to a kid and watching ever so slowly as the insidious liquid of evil seeps into the child's system—through television, movies, video games, comics, difficult life experiences, and lack of love.

That's why I'm always amazed at those who tenaciously cling to that childhood faith. My mother, May Leman, was one such woman. She spent her married life putting up with my dad, who didn't stop drinking until he became a believer in God at age 56. She was a saintly woman who endured a lot. I can't tell you how many times I'd come down the stairs in the morning and see my mom in her favorite chair, praying, with the Bible on her lap. And that was after she'd worked all night in a hospital, helping to hold our family together financially.

I'm always amazed at those who tenaciously cling to that childhood faith.

I was a young jerk who questioned authority and pushed the limits. But even all throughout my teenage years, I could talk with my mother. I respected her. I liked hearing what she had to say. And I knew without a doubt that she believed in her "Cub."

I would have done anything to defend her . . . and I did. I still have a scar on my hand from a guy's front tooth, which just happened to get in front of my fist after he'd said something rotten about my mother.

I smacked him in the face because he told me my mother didn't care about me since she didn't make me change my clothes. You see, in my growing-up days, kids dressed up to go to school, then changed to play clothes when they got home. But I didn't. My mother was the only working mom on the block, so I played in my school clothes.

Stress is a part of life, but we produce the stress. We manufacture it from our life circumstances.

That other child got the message that he was never to talk about my mother in such a way again . . . after I knocked him right off his bike and onto his backside.

If anybody had a reason to be stressed, May Leman did. But she never complained about all the hard work. She did it with a cup-half-full attitude.

Yes, stress is a part of life, but *we* produce the stress. We manufacture it from our life circumstances, then distribute it, so to speak, by "shoulding" on ourselves or other people.

- I *should* have gotten the house cleaned yesterday.
- I *should* get a higher-paying job.
- He *should* care more about me. If he did, life would be easier.
- She *should* help out more around here.
- I *should* lose weight so I look better. Then maybe I'd . . .

We get down on ourselves because we feel we're not good enough. Even the apostle Paul called himself "a wretched man."[5] Well, if he's a wretched man, then what are we? Worse than wretched? Unacceptable? Worthless?

Even if you don't think you're worth it, *nothing* can separate you from the love of God.[6] Not even your own self-doubt. Because God loves you unconditionally, he sent his only Son, Jesus, to die for you. And that makes you worth not only *something* but *everything* to God. Your worth to God—the supreme Creator of the universe—is inestimable, if he would sacrifice his only Son for you.

We all have our down-in-the-dumps, stressed times. We think little of ourselves. We often say yes when we really mean no. We bite off more than we can chew. We create the quandary we find ourselves in by getting involved in far too many activities.

But how often are we still? We live in a society where we are constantly on the go, stressed to the max. I live an incredibly busy life with a lot of travel. But I've also learned how important it is to be still. There's a wonderful Scripture I love: "Be still, and know that I am God."[7]

Psalm 23 says:

> The LORD is my shepherd, I shall not be in
>   want.
>   He makes me lie down in green pastures,
>   he leads me beside quiet waters,
>   he restores my soul.[8]

I've always wondered why the Lord leads beside quiet waters. Why not along raging waters? Wouldn't that show more of God's protection?

I grew up in New York, near where Lake Erie empties into the Niagara River. The current is raging there. Even when I was a kid and as dumb as mud about many things, I knew better than to try to swim in that dangerous river.

When I found out that sheep are apparently afraid of running water, Psalm 23 made a lot more sense to me. Hmm, sheep aren't so different from us, now are they? They like things to be calm and still, and that's when they do the absolute best in life—in a low-stress zone.

Most of the year I live in Tucson, Arizona. The mornings there are glorious, and I love to soak them in. I also love to watch birds. *Well*, I thought one morning, *God takes care of the birds of the field, doesn't he, so why not be a part of feeding them?*

So now I go to Walmart routinely and buy 10-pound bags of thistle seed to stock the bird feeder. Then I go out on the deck with a cup of coffee early in the morning and watch all the little yellow finches that gather at my bird feeder for their breakfast. Whoever coined the expression "free as a bird" is completely off the mark. Birds work their tails off, no pun intended.

But my mornings with the birds remind me profoundly that each day is a gift. So many of us waste our days. We plod through them, doing jobs we hate, and acting like Mr. or Ms. Negativity. We create our own stress. We fail to see the miracles around us—large and small. And we don't see the needs around us either.

My mornings with the birds remind me profoundly that each day is a gift.

When Jesus saw the group of "righteous" folks gathered to stone the woman caught in adultery (I've always wondered: if she was "caught" in the act, then where exactly was the man she was having an affair with?), he had compassion on the woman. Yes, she had done wrong. Yes, she deserved punishment . . . but no more so than all the "righteous" people gathered around her with stones in their hands, who were all hiding their sins.

He just said, "Go and sin no more."

So Jesus started writing in the dirt. We're really not sure what he wrote, but the words caused the accusers to skulk off one at a time and disappear.

Soon it was only Jesus and the woman.

When Jesus had her alone, did he huff and puff and blow her house in like the big, bad wolf would have done?

No, he just said, "Go and sin no more."[9]

With those simple words, Jesus cut straight to the truth—a wonderful ability he had. And with those words, a woman caught in sin was set free to change her life. At that moment, the weight of her sin was lifted—she no longer was burdened by the stresses of her life.

But she also had a choice. You see, Jesus isn't the big, bad wolf who calls out threateningly, "Let me in, or I'll huff, and I'll puff, and I'll blow your house in!"

Instead, Jesus says quietly, "Here I am! I stand at the door and knock. If anyone hears my voice and opens the door, I will come in and eat with him, and he with me."[10]

With those simple words, Jesus cut straight to the truth.

When I was a kid growing up, my mom hung a plaque in my room that showed Jesus knocking at a door. But I didn't notice until years later that there was no doorknob on the outside of that door. It could only be opened from the inside.

Jesus never forces his way into your heart. He simply stands outside the door—always available, waiting, stress-free—for you to decide to open the door.

And if you do open that door, your world changes. You can talk with him anywhere—on the interstate, in the middle of doing the dishes, over lunch, as you watch the moon's reflection at night, or as you watch little finches eating thistle seed at sunrise.

When you begin to rely on him for *all things*, instead of *nothing* or *a few things*, your stress level will go down. Even better, Solomon says your life will be prolonged many years.

The longest-living human we know of was Methuselah, who lived 969 years.[11] I doubt I'll make it that many years, but there's one thing I am determined to do: go about life the very best way I can.

You see, even old guys like me can learn from Mama Pig and the big, bad wolf.

Things to Ponder . . .

"For they will prolong your life many years."
PROVERBS 3:2A

How do you view God? As a wolf huffin' and puffin' at your door? Or as someone gently knocking? How does your experience with your own dad or mom influence how you answer this question?

In what ways might relying on God—for the little things as well as the big things—"prolong your life"?

God loves us . . .
flaws and all.

4

Attention, Walmart Shoppers: Jesus Has Left the Building

And bring you **prosperity**.

PROVERBS 3:2B

Every Thanksgiving season, the Butterball turkey people establish a hotline. If you're a newbie in preparing a turkey and have a question, you can call the 800 number and talk to someone who will tell you what to do with the bird in question.

A lady called the hotline. She'd had a turkey frozen for nine years and wanted to know, "Can I still use it?"

The hotline's answer? "Uh, I better check with my supervisor on that." When back on the line, she said, "It's fine to use it if it's been frozen the entire time—if you're absolutely sure it was never defrosted and your electricity never went out. Then it would be safe to eat."

"Thanks," the lady said. "But I think I'll just give it to a church."

Sadly, that's the way some people think. Give the left-overs to the church or the homeless or the needy or the widowed. That's why you see so many one-dollar bills in the offering plate of a church that has Mercedes and BMWs in the parking lot.

The next time you visit a restaurant, ask your waiter or waitress what their least favorite day of the week to work is. Hands down, they'll say, "Sunday." Why Sunday? Because Christians tend to be cheaper than cheap when it comes to tipping. And on Sunday, after church, that's when all the cheap Christians show up for lunch.

A friend of mine told me about a leader in her church—a man who had a full-time, well-paying job— who would regularly take his family every Sunday after church to whatever car dealership or other business was offering free hot dogs (or other food) and Cokes.

That's how he'd feed his family for lunch. Talk about being cheap.

But we do not serve a Kmart "Blue Light Special" God. Or a Walmart God. He's not discounted. He's not cut-rate.

We do not serve a Kmart "Blue Light Special" God. Or a Walmart God. He's not discounted. He's not cut-rate.

When Jesus did things, he did them right. Jesus would have been a big tipper. He wouldn't have been one of those guys who sheepishly leaves a buck at the table and then walks away.

He would have been more like a guy named Dan Johnston and the people from Springs Church in Winnipeg, Manitoba. I speak literally all over the world to a lot of high-powered audiences, including CEOs, Fortune 500 companies, and some of the biggest churches in America. But when I think of people who do things right, I think of the Canadians at Springs Church.

After doing a fund-raiser in Columbus, Ohio, driving to western New York, then driving to Toronto to catch a nonstop flight, I arrived at midnight in Winnipeg. I was exhausted. But there at the gate was Dan Johnston, who did everything except clip my toenails. He took my bags, opened doors, personally checked me in at the hotel, and made sure everything in my room was satisfactory. Even more, there was a big basket of snacks and goodies in the room, a note from Pastors Leon and Sally Fontaine, and $50 cash in Canadian money for incidentals I might need (since, of course, I would only have American money). They even provided a gift card to Starbucks, since there was one around the corner, in case I needed a caffeine pick-me-up.

That kind of treatment said over and over, "Welcome, welcome, welcome!" Now that's a church that does things right because they have the heart of Jesus. They care about people. Plus they're involved in about every type of ministry a church can be involved in. They meet people where they are (you don't have to clean up to go to that church; you can come as you are). Nobody beats you over the head with the gospel. They simply love you, accept you, and welcome you.

Jesus gave in this lavish sort of way—and more.

When he healed the blind man, did you hear the blind man say, "Hey, I can only see out of my left eye vaguely . . . uh, I think that's an E," when he was given his eye test by the doc? No, the story says this man went from blind to jumping up and down and proclaiming enthusiastically, "I was blind but now I see!"[1] The now-seeing man needed no other proof of who God was. In those days, people who were blind were usually reduced to begging. By opening the man's eyes, Jesus brought him prosperity—the ability to see would now allow him to work and to thrive.

> *The now-seeing man needed no other proof of who God was.*

The account of Jesus' first miracle at Cana in Galilee is one of my favorite stories of all time.[2] Jesus, his disciples, and his mother are at a wedding when the hosts run out of vino. Wine. It was the ultimate embarrassment at a wedding. So what does Mary do?

"Hey, Son, come here," she calls to Jesus. "Do your thing. They're out of wine."

Jesus says, "Woman [note that he calls his mother *woman*, showing his annoyance], what does this have to do with me?" In other words, he's saying a flat-out no.

But Mary's a smart mother. She doesn't say, "What did you say? You ungrateful snot. I gave birth to you when I was 15 years old. Nine hours of labor . . ." Instead she simply turns to the servant and says, "Do whatever my son tells you to do." She takes the proverbial tennis ball of life and serves it squarely back in Jesus' court.

Then something happens. I remember reading the story for the first time and thinking, *Hey, something's wrong here. Something's missing in the story. Jesus clearly says no, but then he goes ahead and changes the water into wine anyway.*

Why? I asked. In my mortal mind, I figured out what must have happened. Mary, Jesus' mother, gave him "the look"—the look you might give your kid if you ask him to do something and he fires back, "No!" (The same kind of look my wife gave me when I purchased 20 bunny rabbits because I thought they'd look cute hopping around our yard.)

I once asked Chuck Swindoll why Jesus changed the water into wine, and he said, "I don't know. Maybe it simply was an uncomfortable position for the host of the wedding to run out of wine at the feast, so Jesus, as a guest, decided to do it."

Or, I wonder, was it because he respected his mother? He didn't have to obey his mother when she asked him to turn the water into wine, but he did. Later, he revealed how much he revered his own mom when he said to the disciple John at the cross, "Take care of Mom."

No matter Jesus' reason, the takeaway of the story is that when the wine is tested, the guy says, "Wow, this is different from most weddings. You saved the top-shelf stuff for the last. This certainly isn't the cheap vino they sell at some convenience stores. This is the best of all."

Jesus did all things perfectly well—including changing the water to wine. But in our humanness, we don't always understand his ways.

Take Mary and Martha, for instance—the women who were upset with Jesus because he took his sweet time to come visit his friend and their brother, Lazarus, who was dying. Jesus seemed to sport an attitude, saying, "I'll get there. Don't worry about it." Yet before he arrives, Lazarus dies. The reproach heaped on him by the grieving sisters is deep.

Then the miracle occurs. Jesus extends his hand toward the tomb and says, "Lazarus, come forth."

And out from the tomb comes this dead dude, still wrapped in the ceremonial cloths that they buried people in. He doesn't just take four steps, take a breath, and then fall over and die again. He walks straight out of that tomb upon Jesus' command!

Yet even though the disciples saw Jesus do these miracles firsthand, they still struggled to believe he was indeed the long-awaited Messiah. The Bible says they "put their faith in him"[3] after the first miracle in Cana, but that didn't mean they didn't have doubts.

If you have trouble believing in God, you're not alone. Even the disciples who walked and talked with Jesus had trouble. They saw God's awesome power close-up in his Son, but it was still hard to get their mortal minds around it.

When Jesus gathered his disciples in the upper room for a last meal together, he told them, "Hey, guys, I'm outta here. I'm going to prepare a place for you, and you know where I'm going."

I love Thomas, because he was so stupid he reminds me of myself. He said, "Lord, we don't have the foggiest idea what you're talking about."

Philip got into the act next. "Yeah, show us the Father, and then we'll know."

So Jesus said to Philip, "After all this time you've been with me, you don't know who I am? If you've seen me, you've seen the Father."[4]

Even with this clarification, his disciples still didn't get it. And when times got intense, they went belly-up.

They failed. Judas betrayed Jesus, then committed suicide. Peter denied Jesus three times, then wept bitterly. Others ran away and hid, afraid they would meet the same fate as Jesus.

Yet Jesus forgave them. He gave all but Judas, who was dead, a second chance to prove their loyalty to him. And the next time, they didn't fail. In fact, most of them were martyred for their faith.

If you have trouble believing in God, you're not alone. Even the disciples who walked and talked with Jesus had trouble.

You see, God and his Son, Jesus, are the only perfect ones. We humans are human. None of us belongs on a pedestal. We fail. We feel guilty. We beat ourselves up about it. The only sinless man was Jesus.

Jesus always did the right thing—not the expedient or cheap thing. If we do the same, we will prosper in the end.

"Bring the whole tithe into the storehouse, that there may be food in my house. Test me in this," says the LORD Almighty, "and see if I will not throw open the floodgates of heaven and pour out so much blessing that you will not have room enough for it."[5]

This is the statement of a lavish God, who is ready to pour out his blessing upon us . . . but we also must have God's lavish heart.

Ever hear someone say, "If there is a God, why does he allow people to starve in Africa?" I want to shoot back the question, "Why do *you* allow it?" You see, God uses ordinary people to do extraordinary things in others' lives. And you can be a part of that—in a small or large way.

But it takes stepping outside yourself, taking a risk, and looking for others' needs. So many of us complain about what we don't have instead of acknowledging what we do have and thanking God for those blessings.

We humans are human. None of us belongs on a pedestal.

Each day is a gift, but how we spend that gift is up to us. Gifts and talents should never be used only for ourselves.

I believe wholeheartedly in something I call *natural tithing*. If you see a need in someone's life and you can meet it right then, do it. If you can do it anonymously, all the better. For example, if a person needs a meal, and you have seven bucks in your pocket and can buy him a Big Mac at McDonald's, complete with fries and a Coke, do so. (Or, for a lower cholesterol version, try Subway.) Give a little, and you'll be amazed at how your own perspective on life will improve. The famous coach John Wooden said, "You can't live a perfect day without doing something for someone who will never be able to repay you."[6]

> *If you see a need in someone's life and you can meet it right then, do it.*

Although I always strive to do the right thing, I find myself, like Saint Paul, sometimes doing what I don't want to do: Bypassing the needy when I'm in a rush. Brushing off those who rub me the wrong way. Or thinking, *What if that person uses the money to buy a cheap bottle of muscatel instead of food?* What others do with what you give them is up to them. What's up to you is learning to have the heart of a natural tither—a lavish giver.

Let's face it: we're all flawed to the core. There are some people you'll like and feel comfortable with; there are others you'll have a hard time liking, much less loving.

But Jesus said, "Whatever you did for one of the least of these brothers of mine, you did for me."[7] If we remember that every person is a creation of Almighty God and turn our hearts toward natural tithing, God will bring us prosperity of heart, mind, and finances so we can lavish even more on others.

When we do the right thing, not the expedient or cheap thing, we become more like Jesus, who gave lavishly.

Now that's indeed something you can take to the bank . . . eternally.

Things to Ponder . . .

"And bring you prosperity."
PROVERBS 3:2B

What does *prosperity* mean to you? Money? Health? Family? Friends? Position? Why?

What truly makes you happy? What could you do to make someone you know happy?

Thank God for his blessings . . . and then bless others.

Each day is a gift,
but how we spend it is up to us.

5

I'm All Yours—All 96 Percent!

Let **love and faithfulness** never leave
you; bind them around your neck.

PROVERBS 3:3A

The scene in a Tucson, Arizona, park on a beautiful summer day was anything but usual—even though it seemed that way at first. Two women met by a park bench to have lunch together. One of the women set an infant carrier with a baby between them. The other slightly younger woman cooed at the baby and gently rocked her as they ate their sack lunches and talked.

Toward the end of their time together, an elderly gentleman—a grandpa type—walked up to them during his stroll around the park and commented on how beautiful the baby was. Then he asked, "Who's the lucky mom?"

The two women looked at each other . . . and both women's eyes filled with happy tears. They didn't know what to say.

You see, one was the adoptive mother, the other was the birth mother. They had just been on a radio show with me, talking about the great gift of adoption and what an incredible expression of love it really is—from both sides.

Love by itself is not enough, because love wears thin.

The adoptive mother had opened her arms and heart wide to receive someone else's child as her own to love for a lifetime.

The birth mother had loved her child so much that she thought more about the welfare of the baby than about herself. She decided to offer that child for adoption so the baby would be loved, be cared for, and receive opportunities that the young birth mother would not be able to provide.

The radio show had been poignant—a powerful expression of love that brought tears to the eyes of many people listening, including myself.

These two women provided a life lesson in what the concepts of love and faithfulness are all about.

Love by itself is not enough, because love wears thin. We can think, *If I just love my child enough, everything will turn out okay*, but nothing is further from the truth. If you *just* love your child, you'll end up with a little monster on your hands. Love and discipline are inseparable. If you love *and* discipline your kid, then everything will most likely work out all right.

Love is not two young lovers entwined in each other's arms, gazing moonstruck at the lake on a summer night. If you simply love your spouse, it's not enough for the long haul. All the experts agree that the moony-eyed love—the honeymoon effect—lasts about two years. So what do you do between then and 48 years later, when you get your picture in the newspaper for your fiftieth anniversary and you both look wrinkled up like raisins?

You must choose to love. You must be faithful to love. Those who say love is a decision are right on the mark. It's easy to love when the person is lovable. But the blessing is in loving that person even when he or she isn't lovable. If you commit to love your spouse and remain faithful for a lifetime, then you have a bond that won't be broken by any hardship or threats of divorce. Love and faithfulness mean thinking of another's needs first, before your own.

Those who say love is a decision are right on the mark.

When our teenage daughter Lauren invited a kid to go to a ball game with us, I asked her why.

"Because nobody likes him, Dad," she said.

Wow. That was a gut check on my own attitude (I didn't like the kid much either).

Lauren had already learned something important about love and faithfulness. As Proverbs 3:3 says, they should never leave you. Love and faithfulness should be such a part of your character that they're bound "around your neck."

When you show love and faithfulness, you stand out in a fickle, faithless world where everyone is out to protect number one—themselves. That's why we read with such interest stories of heroes and heroines in the newspaper and online. Tales of people who have made a difference because they chose to risk their lives to save others. They're the down-to-earth, good people that God has called each of us to be.

We all exert faith in different forms, whether we're people of faith or not. For example, when you drive through a green light, you exercise faith that you will be able to proceed without someone hitting you—that other people will pay attention to the red light as they are approaching the intersection. You are faithful to go to your job every day . . . or else you won't have a job. You are faithful to love your spouse . . . and to turn away advances from others who might seem more "attractive."

We all exert faith in different forms, whether we're people of faith or not.

Are there people who are unfaithful? Yes, scads of them. You can credit the high divorce rate in part to unfaithfulness. But blessed are he and she who are faithful and honor their marriage vows. Blessed are the ones who do life right—who choose to love and be faithful.

I love the saying "Trust God. All Others Pay Cash." That's because God is the only one who won't fail us. People will—even those we love the most. We love to put sports figures, movie stars, musicians, and pastors on a pedestal. But the only thing they can do is fall off that pedestal, because none of them is perfect.

Faith in God is what will carry us through the tough times. Faith is believing when we can't see the end result.

> Now faith is being sure of what we hope for and certain of what we do not see.[1]

Jesus was always faithful to his mission. During the time he walked the earth, he revealed who he was and is through everything he did—turning the water to wine, healing the blind man, raising Lazarus from the dead, feeding the multitudes with only five loaves of bread and two fish from a young boy's lunch.

As human beings, sometimes we're faithful and loving; sometimes we're not. However, when we don't do the right thing, we shouldn't simply beat ourselves up about it. That won't help us or the other person. Instead, we should ask for forgiveness. If we make the apology, life goes on. Perhaps not in the same way if it was a large breach of trust, but all we can do is make the effort.

So when you mess up, fess up to it. This applies to all areas of life—whether a marriage, any other relationship, or a business partnership.

I am thankful every day for my mother's unshakable faith in God . . . and in me. She was convinced her little "Cub" would make it—even when I didn't know if I'd make it. Behind the scenes she continued to pray for me (and I'd like to point out that she had good reason to pray for me on a number of fronts). She was loving and faithful. She never gave up.

Neither did Jesus, even when the disciples were as dumb as mud. When they were all in a boat and a big storm came up at sea, the disciples panicked. They woke up Jesus, terrified that they were all going to die.

Jesus' response? He was perturbed. "You woke me up. Why? Because there's a small storm? Oh, you of little faith."[2]

Whether you are a person of faith or not, you will go through storms in life. So what was Jesus saying by his response?

Here's the Leman translation: "Being a Christian doesn't guarantee you a 'get out of jail free' pass from life's storms. However, if you believe in me, then I will be with you always, even to the ends of the earth."[3]

God's not interested in playing Make a Deal with you. In fact, he's *never* interested in *any* deal.

"What deal is that?" you say.

The same deal I tried to make with God all my life, before my mom's faith caught up with me: "Lord, I'm yours. You got me. All 96 percent."

With God, it's 100 percent or nothing: 100 percent trust, 100 percent commitment, 100 percent of your heart.

God doesn't want 96 percent of your life. He wants *all of you*.

But there's a promise associated with that too—a better deal than you can ever get with any human being. James 4:8 says that when you choose to move close to God, he comes closer to you. But as the bumper sticker says, "If you feel far away from God, guess who moved?"

That puts the onus on us. What is the Scripture really saying? "I'll become real to you and fellowship with you, but it's your move. You've got to move toward me. And when you choose to do so, you'll know my love and faithfulness are never-ending."

Things to Ponder . . .

"Let love and faithfulness never leave you;
bind them around your neck."

PROVERBS 3:3A

Put your iPod earphones on and you'll hear nothing. But flip the "on" switch and the sudden blaring of sound will surround you.

For anything productive to happen between you and your Maker, guess who has to flip the switch?

You.

God's love and faithfulness surround you
and are free for the taking.

6

The Marines (and God)
Need a Few Good Men . . .
and Women

Then you will win favor and **a good name** in the sight of God and man.

For years I've known Jerry Kindall, a former major league baseball player who won the American League Championship with the Minnesota Twins. He was also the head baseball coach at the University of Arizona, where he won three national titles in college ball. Like most athletes who win championships, he's got a ring that could choke a horse. It's huge. When you see it, you can't miss it.

One day I ran into Jerry's wife. She was wearing a beautiful diamond pendant.

"Wow," I said, "that's a lovely necklace."

"Oh," she said happily, "didn't I tell you about that? My Jerry gave it to me."

As God is my judge, instinctively I knew where that pendant came from. "Not the ring," I said.

She nodded. "The ring."

Jerry had taken his championship ring to the jeweler, had the diamond removed to make a necklace for his wife, then melted down the ring and made four pins for his children.

Later, when I saw Jerry, I asked, "Jerry, how could you do that?" I was still in shock. I know professional athletes are all competitive people who want to win, and that ring is a symbol of winning. That's why I cringed when I first heard about it. I still have my intramural plaque, and this guy melts down his ring?

He smiled. "It's actually one of the easier things I've done in my life. One day I was sitting in church, playing with the ring and admiring it. That's when I knew I needed to share it with those I loved the most."

Wow, I thought, *talk about a low ego.*

Some of the guys who win championship rings wear them so everyone can see them. But not Jerry. He's a salt-of-the-earth kind of guy. A guy who puts the ones he loves first . . . a guy whose name brings smiles and nods wherever he goes because of the integrity behind it.

Contrast him with Bernie Madoff, the American stockbroker who started out with $5,000 from his savings as a sprinkler installer and lifeguard and rose quickly as an investment advisor and the executive chairman of the NASDAQ stock market. He gained entrance to the top echelons in Washington and contributed to Democratic campaigns. He donated approximately $6 million to lymphoma research and numerous other charities.

But in 2009, Madoff pleaded guilty to 11 federal felonies and admitted to turning his wealth management business into a massive Ponzi scheme that defrauded thousands of investors of billions of dollars—almost $65 billion. He'd even defrauded his own family.[1]

Madoff may have had a great name in the sight of man—at least for a while—but underneath it all he was bilking everyone of money. And after all his efforts, what legacy does this man leave? One of shame for his family and friends. His name will forever be connected to a long-lived Ponzi scheme, while his donations to charities will be downplayed or mentioned with embarrassment because it wasn't even his money.

> *We men and women are shortsighted. We can be easily fooled.*

It's easy to have a good name in the sight of man. That's because we men and women are shortsighted. We can be easily fooled (but not children—they're pretty perceptive).

That's why Proverbs 3:4 is so profound. It doesn't say you'll have a good name just "in the sight of man." It says "in the sight of God and man." No matter what you do, you can't fool God. But if you focus on pleasing God, you gain a good name all around—in the sight of both God and man.

How much does having a good name mean to you?

When I think of a good name, I think immediately of two people who were instrumental early on in my career.

One is Bob Svob, who was influential in helping me build my career. When I was head dorm rat, he spotted something in me. He plucked me out of the residence hall system, entrusting me with becoming an assistant dean of students. I worked under him for 10 years, and in those 10 years, I never heard anybody say a single bad thing about Bob Svob. (But I could give you the zip codes of all the people who don't like me.) Bob was a salt-of-the-earth person, a hard worker if there ever was one, who always did the right thing and always reminded me that we had to do things right and treat people in a fair manner.

Stupid me, one day I meandered into his office and sat down. "Dean, I'm having some trouble," I said, then went on to lay out a plethora of problems I was facing. I was, after all, the administrator of the "code of conduct," so I dealt with all the idiotic things that college students do. And then I had to deal with the attorneys who defended the students and the university attorney who served as prosecutor.

Do you know what Bob's comment was, after he heard my long litany?

How much does having a good name mean to you?

"Well, Kevin, if you didn't have these problems, I wouldn't have needed to employ you, would I?"

That put things in perspective for me, a young buck of 29 starting off in my career. I never forgot his words. Although he said them kindly, they made me feel about as smart as a pet rock. *Yeah, duh, you're right.*

Bob always had the ability to cut straight through any blather to the truth of the matter. But he was also an encourager—he took time to tell you when you did a good job.

Today, at 93, he's still an encourager. I was at his house recently for a barbecue, and the first thing he did was encourage me. "Regulation Bob," as we called him back at the university, still runs two miles a day and plays golf three to four times a week. He always hits the ball down the center of the golf course. He's rarely in the rough. And he's still reminding people to do the right thing—always. Bob has maintained his good name in the sight of God and man.

The other man in the office with Bob was Bill Foster, the associate dean of students. He was the man I directly reported to. Behind the scenes, he was the one who made everything happen for me to become a dean of students. He saw something in me that told him I'd do well in that role at a major university.

Bill loves to tell the story about one of the other head residents who complained, "Leman is too close to the students." We laughed about that complaint a few weeks ago over Mexican food.

Problem is, people think you have to maintain distance to be in authority over kids. But Jesus was always personal with people, wasn't he? He loved them, then went right to the heart of the matter with the personal touch. He was all about a personal relationship.

Jesus was always personal with people.

In society today, we train pastors not to get too close to the flock, to maintain a safe distance. Yet when you think about people you really admire and love, what is it about them that makes them so attractive to you? They take a personal interest in you.

Because of people like Bob and Bill, I discovered that the relationship—the connection—is what makes respect and integrity flourish so that others want to listen to what you have to say. And then, because of your good name and your consistency, people put their trust in you.

Back when I was working with Bob and Bill, the way I dealt with students established the pattern for my life.

When Bill turned 85, for fun I spilled 85 silver dollars and dropped a birthday card in the entranceway of his home. I will never forget the good name of Bill Foster, who became more like a father to me at the university than a co-worker and boss, and whose legacy of being personal has carried on through me.

If there's one word that encapsulates what I do on my Facebook page, it's *personal*. I'm personal with people. I've always been personal with people. I take an interest in them and what they're doing. I bet that this week alone, I gave away 12 books after talking with individuals, since I thought the books could be a help to them. If you think that's no big deal, this might help your perspective. People always assume that authors get free books. But they often pay 50 percent of the retail cost to buy their own book. So if an author gives you a book, it's likely they have paid for it. But I do it because I love seeing the smiles on people's faces, and I also like helping people and seeing families succeed.

Recently I gave a graduating football player my book *The Way of the Shepherd* (coauthored with William

Pentak) because he decided he wants to go into coaching. I told him, "This little book is loaded with principles that will work in any life situation you're put in."

He thanked me up and down.

Now, will he read, study, and use the book? I have no idea. I hope he does. I believe that if you've been blessed in life, materially or otherwise, you should bless others. If you don't, I have to ask, "What's wrong with you? Don't you understand that the gifts you're given come from your Maker?"

All of us need to stop and think, *Who believed in me?* Which people, like Bob and Bill for me, have influenced your life, character, name, and direction?

> *If you've been blessed in life, materially or otherwise, you should bless others. If you don't, I have to ask, "What's wrong with you?"*

Some of you could list those people on one hand, or you might even have trouble coming up with a couple. Others of you are already starting to scribble your long list.

But even if no one believes in you with all your imperfections and shortcomings, God, your Creator, does.

A lot of people have good names in the sight of man through their notoriety in business, sports—you name it. But when those people die, what fame do they really have? Is it fleeting, or do they have a relationship with their Maker? If you've met the living God up close and personal and you've made that commitment to serve him for the rest of your life, then your good name has already been established in God's eyes. If you haven't, then nothing you've gained will go with you to your life beyond the grave.

The older you get, the more acutely aware you become of how fast the sands of time are flying by.

So how do you win favor and a good name in the sight of both God and man? By showing kindness, love, and compassion. Life is short, and the older you get, the more acutely aware you become of how fast the sands of time are flying by.

But I want to clarify something here. Note that Proverbs 3:4 says, "A good name." It doesn't say, "A perfect name." God isn't interested in the "perfect you," because there's no such thing this side of heaven. He's interested in the "good you." A good person can still mess up. But what you do with that mess—how you respond to it—makes all the difference in the world. Do you suck it up and admit your mistake, ask for forgiveness, and move on? Or do you wallow in that mistake until you're sucked down into the mud? Or maybe you point fingers at others: *I wouldn't have done that if she hadn't made me*; or, *The reason I'm not a success in life is because he did me wrong.*

Winners in life—those who have a good name in the sight of God and man—take rejection and failure and use them as stepping-stones to success in life.

God isn't interested in the "perfect you." . . . He's interested in the "good you."

John Wooden was a revered UCLA basketball coach who held the respect of everyone. He lived to be 99 years of age. Interestingly, he never told his team to win; instead, he emphasized playing the game the way it needed to be played.

He was a man of few words, but the words he spoke were carefully chosen. They live on as a legacy of his good name.

Just listen to some of his gems:

Be more concerned with your character than your reputation, because your character is what you really are, while your reputation is merely what others think you are.[2]

Things turn out best for the people who make the best out of the way things turn out.[3]

Talent is God-given. Be humble. Fame is man-given. Be grateful. Conceit is self-given. Be careful.[4]

You can't live a perfect day without doing something for someone who will never be able to repay you.[5]

Never make excuses. Your friends don't need them and your foes won't believe them.[6]

It is amazing how much can be accomplished if no one cares who gets the credit.[7]

Ability may get you to the top, but it takes character to keep you there.[8]

Pick out one of those quotes today and try to live it out. If you do, within the week, your life—and the lives of myriad others around you—will be transformed. And you'll be on your way to a good name in the sight of both God and man.

I guarantee it.

Things to Ponder . . .

*"Then you will win favor and a good name
in the sight of God and man."*

PROVERBS 3:4

What's the difference between a "good you" and a "perfect you"? Why do you think God would be interested in one and not the other?

If you could leave behind one legacy on earth, what would it be?

*Better to be a person with character . . .
than to be a character.*

7

You're the Potter, I'm the Clay . . . But I Do Have a Few Suggestions

Trust in the LORD with all your heart.

PROVERBS 3:5A

I grew up in a lower-middle-class home, with parents who didn't have two nickels to rub together. My mom especially didn't have an easy life. She was a working mom in a day and neighborhood where all the other moms were stay-at-home June Cleavers.

But my mom had something a lot of the other moms didn't have. Trust and belief. She trusted in God even when times were hard. She trusted that all three of her kids would follow the path God was sending them on. And she believed in me—even when she didn't have any good reason to believe I'd turn out to be anything. Me? I did my best for years to duck out of contact with anything that reeked of Christianity.

But when my mom caught up with me and dragged me to church and insisted I sit with her, I'd hear over and over again the music to the hymn "Trust and Obey" wheezed out by the old lady who manned the rickety organ. To this day, the words "Trust and obey, for there's no other way to be happy in Jesus, but to trust and obey"[1] are stuck in my memory.

The church I go to today is a far cry from the simple upbringings of my mother's church. It's more like rock and roll Saturday night. You won't hear many hymns; you'll hear praise music and the twang of guitars and the rumble of drums. But I sometimes miss the simplicity and beauty of the old hymns that were loaded with such powerful words, even when I wasn't crazy about hearing them.

You see, for all my running away from May Leman's faith, in the end, her trust in God caught up with me . . . and it stuck. And since then I've passed on my mom's trust in God to my own children as well. May Leman is now in heaven, but her legacy continues on earth—through myself, my kids, and now my grandkids.

> *Her trust in God caught up with me . . . and it stuck.*

There are two sides to trust—giving it and receiving it. If you have trust in God now, it's because somebody before you trusted God with all their heart, then made an impact on your life. Perhaps now would be a good time to return the favor—to contribute to someone else's life in the same way by role-modeling what trusting God looks like.

But when you do that, don't forget to do it with all your heart.

And therein lies the problem. I've already referred to it earlier as *developmental carnality*. It's the battle of wills within yourself that Saint Paul himself referred to in a letter to the Romans: "I don't understand myself. I tell myself I won't do these things, but I do them"

(Leman translation).[2] Talk about a perfect statement of the human condition that all of us struggle with. If we know what the right thing to do is, then why don't we do it?

Because within us there is a continual testing of wills. We pray the Lord's Prayer, "Your will be done on earth as it is in heaven,"[3] but the reality is easier said than done. Why? Because God gave us a brain, gifts, skills, and free will. The idea of being submissive to anything or anyone, including God, is downright threatening to a lot of us.

If we know what the right thing to do is, then why don't we do it?

The struggle is all about relinquishing control. We all have our insecurities we want to hang on to. Our natural inclination is not to let go of the control of our lives. "God," we say, "I know you're the Potter, I'm the clay . . . but I do have a few suggestions."

It's like the kid who is trying to dive off a diving board into a pool for the first time. Does he want to dive into the pool? Yeah. Why doesn't he? Because he's fearful.

You can always tell when it's a kid's first time, because he'll pace back and forth—up on the board, back down to the concrete around the pool, then back to the board. He'll let other kids pass him in line.

But once that kid, for whatever reason, determines to make that dive and get his face wet, often he'll take to water like a fish. I've watched that process firsthand in both of my grandchildren, and now they swim like little fish.

Let's take the analogy further. Either we can pursue excellence in life by taking that leap off the diving board, or we can sit on the edge of the pool, watching life go by. A third option is simply to tread water, doing what we need to do day in and day out to survive, but never experiencing the thrill of jumping off the board.

Where are you right now?

- Are you taking that leap off the board? Really enjoying life and living it as it should be lived, focusing on relationships and making a difference in the lives of others?

- Are you sitting at the side of the pool, watching life go by, wishing it weren't so boring? Are you wasting the life God has granted you?

- Are you treading water, just trying to keep your head above the waves because life feels too overwhelming to make a change?

Few people are taking the leap off the board. The majority of people are sitting at the side of the pool or treading water. That's why *American Idol* and other reality shows are such a draw. People don't like the life they're living, so they need to live their life through someone else's experience. And waiting to see which person is the next to get booted off the show is the highlight of their week.

> *Life is temporal; it won't last. But shouldn't that idea kick us into full gear rather than sideline us?*

Life is temporal; it won't last. But shouldn't that idea kick us into full gear rather than sideline us? In what area do you want to make a difference? Then why aren't you doing it?

It all comes down to trust, doesn't it? *If I venture into this area, what if I fail? What if people laugh at me?*

So what if you do fail? So what if people do laugh? Will the world end? Or will you get up tomorrow morning and brush your teeth like you always do?

If you trust in God with all your heart, you don't need to fear any earthly failure because your position in heaven is secure.

But could your fear have to do with more than not trusting God? Could it have something to do with what I call the "deception of perfection"? We touched on it a bit in the last chapter, but I want to talk about it again, since it's a huge issue that holds people back from living the life they want to live and from trusting God with all their heart.

When I'm doing seminars, I often ask my audience a question: "How many of you have drawings on your refrigerator door that little kids—whether your own or someone else's—have done?"

After a show of hands, I ask, "Well, are those pictures any good?"

Then I answer myself, using a Grandma voice. "Excuse me, Dr. Leman, they're downright precious. My grandson Timmy drew that picture for his grandma. It's an airplane."

"Uh, ma'am," I say, "I talked to little Timmy about it. It's a dinosaur."

"Oh, well, it's still precious," Grandma claims.

I agree. The picture might not be perfect, but it is precious.

That's the way God looks at us—as an imperfect picture that isn't quite all together, but very precious.

But so many of us turn around and say, "Well, God, you're the Potter, I'm the clay. Mold me, use me. I'm yours, Lord . . . well, except for my 401(k). I want to hang on to that and take care of it myself, if you don't mind."

> *"God, you're the Potter, I'm the clay. Mold me, use me. I'm yours, Lord . . . well, except for my 401(k)."*

But the Bible tells us we serve a jealous God. He doesn't want just what we're willing to give him. He wants us to trust him with all our heart, with all our life, and with all our possessions.

"If you love me," he says, "then trust me, and do what my Scripture tells you to do."

It's so hard to pull over and let God get behind the wheel of our life's car, isn't it, when we're so used to driving it ourselves?

I do okay with letting God have control for a while. Then I say, "You know, Lord, it's a beautiful day. Let me drive for a while."

So I take over the driver's seat, push God to the passenger seat, and take off full tilt.

Two miles down the road of life, I crash.

The first word out of my mouth is, "Lord . . ."

"That you, Leman?" God says.

"Yup," I say. "Do you think you could call me a tow truck? I just ran off the road and dinged up my car."

"It's on the way, fat boy."

God is able to keep us from sinning if we trust him and let him take control.

How many times do we have to go through the back-and-forth of relinquishing control before we understand? Sometimes I shake my head at myself because I'm all too human, and I learn far too slowly.

All of us are needy. Not one of us is perfect. But we're all told to have trusting, childlike faith.

I remember my mom talking often to me about having Jesus in my heart. One day when I was about five years old, we were having

> *I take over the driver's seat, push God to the passenger seat, and take off full tilt. Two miles down the road of life, I crash.*

lunch, and I said, "If Jesus is in my heart, does he get wet when I drink my milk?"

Apparently I didn't understand physiology very well.

But note that I didn't question the existence of Jesus. I didn't try to argue it away. I accepted that he was in my heart. And I simply asked a question in childlike faith to try to understand him better.

In today's complicated world, there is one simple choice we can make that will take all the stress out of our trying to be in the driver's seat of life: "Trust and obey, for there's no other way to be happy in Jesus, but to trust and obey."

Things to Ponder . . .

"Trust in the LORD with all your heart."
PROVERBS 3:5A

When are you most likely to nudge God over and take the wheel like a NASCAR driver?

The old children's song "Jesus Loves Me" includes the lyrics "I am weak, but he is strong." Are you living your life like "he is weak, but I am strong"? That's called the *human delusion.* What are you going to do to change?

Trust isn't a one-shot deal.
It's an ongoing relationship.

8

God Doesn't Want to Be Your #1

And lean not on your own **understanding**.

PROVERBS 3:5B

Have you ever heard the saying, "God said it. I believe it. And that settles it"?

I always do a double take when I hear that. Blithe statements like that drive me a little bit crazy. Did God create us as thinking individuals or as automatons who merely fall into line like little ducks behind Papa or Mama Duck? God wants us to understand who he is—not just to believe something or do something because he said it and we're forced to believe it.

God's style, though, is not *authoritarian*. He doesn't get his way by scaring the bejeebies out of you—grabbing you by the scruff of the neck or twisting your earlobes and then threatening, "You better get it together, or else. . . ." He doesn't say, "I'll strike you with lightning if you question me. How dare you! I'm in charge. I'm *always* in charge. So believe what I say. Don't ask any questions. You're a mere, lowly human, the dust under my feet. You will do exactly what I tell you to do."

God also isn't *permissive*. He doesn't say, "Oh dear, did you mess up again? Let's get a Band-Aid to fix you right up so you can go back out there on your own." He's not a Disneyland God who says, "Oh, you're short on cash this month? I'll whip up a lottery win for you." He isn't a laissez-faire, anything-goes God you can treat like a vending machine for goodies.

No, God is *authoritative.* He doesn't twist your earlobe or your arm and say, "You *must* acknowledge me." He simply is the supreme authority in all things, the ruler of heaven and the ruler of this earth. The God before whom every knee shall bow!

For we will all stand before God's judgment seat. It is written:

> "As surely as I live," says the Lord,
> "every knee will bow before me;
>> every tongue will confess to God."[1]

He is a God who is to be feared in a healthy way because of who he is.

> The fear of the LORD is the beginning of
>> wisdom;
>> all who follow his precepts have good
>> understanding.
> To him belongs eternal praise.[2]

It's clear that by following God's principles—his rules, even though many of us chafe at that word—we will gain good understanding. We will be wise.

Proverbs 3:5 says, "Trust in the LORD with all your heart and lean not on your own understanding." When we trust in people, all they can do is fall off their pedestal.

There's a wonderful saying: "If you see a turtle at the top of a fence post, he didn't get there by himself." By ourselves, we human beings are not very smart. A peek at a newspaper heading or the stories of the day online proves how many messes we can get ourselves into. And none of us—even the smartest man in the world—is immune.

> *If you see a turtle at the top of a fence post, he didn't get there by himself.*

But if you acknowledge who God is—the Creator of the universe, your Maker who knows you far better than you know yourself—and you choose not to lean on your own understanding but to seek after God, you will be at "the beginning of wisdom." There's no better deal than that!

But we human beings like things in little packages, like those Christian fish on the backs of cars and the numerous cute sayings people come up with. Has anyone ever said to you, "God is #1 in my life"?

Sounds "religious" and good, doesn't it? At least on the surface.

Well, God doesn't want to be your #1. God isn't a number, and he doesn't need a number. God is God. He's on a different plane than you, his creation. Saying "God is my #1" is trying to retain the reins of control by categorizing him as belonging to you. He is the Alpha (the beginning) and the Omega (the ending) of all, and you're not even in his league.

Today's society smacks of irreverence. God's name is used in times of frustration or anger. But is that really the way you should address the highest supreme being in the universe? Or the kind of attention you want from God Almighty? After all, when someone calls my name, I turn my head and pay attention. When you call the name of God, he turns his head and you get his attention.

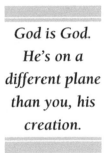

God is God. He's on a different plane than you, his creation.

Perhaps we should all get a healthy dose of fear by taking the time to understand who God is. Our own perspective of him—tainted by our previous experiences with so-called godly people—isn't enough. The only way to gain true understanding of him is by reading his words in the Bible and by choosing to have a personal relationship with him. After all, you can't get to know anyone without learning about their background, who they are, and what their mission is, can you?

Imagine that Jesus is coming to your hometown today. No one but you knows of his plans, because you are the one person he wants to visit with. You'll have an entire day to ask God in the flesh every question you've ever had about faith, creation, the mysteries of the universe, why good things happen to bad people and bad things happen to good people, and so many quandaries that you've wrestled with for years.

Imagine that Jesus is coming to your hometown today.

After your day with Jesus, what do you think your faith would be like?

"Well, my faith would be unshakable," you might say. "I'd be on fire for God. I'd be unstoppable."

You fool. You'd go belly-up in no time, just like the disciples did. It's called the human condition. That's because, when you count on your own understanding alone, it's far easier to fall into doubt. To go back to your old patterns of unwise choices or simply sitting on the fence.

If the disciples, who walked and talked with Jesus every day, didn't understand who Jesus really was, what makes you think you'd be any different?

Doubting Thomas always gets the shaft for doubting—for having to place his fingers in the nail imprints on Jesus' hand to believe that Jesus did indeed rise from the grave. But weren't all the disciples in the same boat of doubt?

And don't we all find it easy to doubt today? I always liked the disciples, because they're similar to me. Thick in the head. Falling continually short in their understanding when trying to comprehend weighty things.

We human beings tend to beat ourselves up. We hear "religious" folks tout miracles (with the promise of delivery if we donate "only" a hundred bucks to that smiling, suavely coiffed televangelist), and we expect miracles too. But then they don't come. We're in the same slimy place we were the day before: our kids are mouthy, our marriage is a mess, there's no job on the horizon that can dig us out of debt.

So many people pray and feel like they don't get answers or results. But their prayers are more like the speculative faith of a door-to-door salesman: *If I knock on enough doors, somebody's going to open one and I'll make a sale.*

But if you are trusting in the Lord with all your heart and leaning not on your own understanding, then you're not halfway committed. You're all-the-way committed.

And being all-the-way committed means you trust God to take control . . . *and you let go.*

You completely hand the reins of your life over to the very God who loves, cares for, and watches over each of us individually. He knows you and calls you by name.

So many people pray and feel like they don't get answers or results.

You're not merely one of the billions of humans populating this earth. He knows every move you make, every thought you have . . . even the random ones before you have your coffee in the morning.

So, let me ask you, if God is really who he says he is—the Creator of the entire universe and everything in it—then why are we acting like he can't help us with the problems we face? Is it because we truly don't understand who God is? Or how much we mean to him? Or how much he wants the best for us?

If the King of Kings and Lord of Lords loves you, but you put yourself down and say you're not good enough to have a relationship with him, how much sense does that make? Aren't you putting down the very person he created, sent his Son Jesus to die for, and thinks has inestimable value? He calls you his child—his son, his daughter. You are the son or daughter of the King of the universe!

So then why aren't you acting like it?

There's a wonderful little Scripture in the Song of Solomon:

> Catch for us the little foxes,
>   the little foxes
> that ruin the vineyards,
>   our vineyards that are in bloom.[3]

What little foxes in your life are ruining your vineyard—the vineyard that would otherwise be in bloom in your life? Why are the grapes that you harvest not what they should be—or could be? What issues are you letting control your life or not dealing with? What little things are separating you from the love of God and from furthering your understanding about what a majestic God he is?

When you truly grasp who God is, everything about your life changes. Just think, it's now illegal in many states to talk on your cell phone while driving down the interstate and through a city. But at any time and at any place you can talk to the God of the universe. In fact, he's waiting for you to make the connection.

He is the authoritative God of the universe before whom every knee in heaven and on earth shall one day bow. Yet his eyes are focused lovingly on you, waiting to hear from you.

However, God is a gentleman. Even with all his authority, he will never force you into a decision to trust him—to turn your life over to him. He merely asks you gently to trust him and to always seek to understand him, so you can have a growing, personal relationship with him for all eternity.

Once you understand who God is, you begin that marvelous journey toward an unshakable, unstoppable, passionate faith that will transform your life and unmistakably influence those around you.

So don't fall for the "God said it. I believe it. And that settles it for me" lingo. You deserve more than that.

So does Almighty God.

Things to Ponder . . .

"And lean not on your own understanding."

PROVERBS 3:5B

If Jesus came to visit you today, what questions would you ask him?

How might choosing to believe in God—instead of your own understanding—change what's on your plate for today?

> *God doesn't want you to*
> *throw him a bone.*
> *He wants the whole enchilada.*

9

God Is Not Your Copilot

In all your ways **acknowledge him**.

PROVERBS 3:6A

Some of the best things I've learned about God, I've learned through the humorous old movie *Oh, God!* Back in the late 1960s, there was a movement of people who believed "God is dead." And that movement spawned this movie in the late 1970s. John Denver plays the main character, a grocery store assistant manager who questions God's existence. So God in the flesh (played by comedian George Burns) chooses John Denver to tell the world that he isn't dead.

Immediately all these weird things start happening to Denver. He's completely confused and more than a little unnerved. When he at last meets George Burns—"God"—their conversation goes something like this:

> "If you are God, prove it to me."

"Okay, if you're God, do something God-like," Denver says.

"Oh, you mean like change the weather?" Burns says.

"Yeah," Denver says. "Make it rain."

All of a sudden, it starts to rain in the car. And *only* in the car.

Denver says in awe, "You are God."[1]

What was his real request? "If you are God, prove it to me."

The people who walked the earth the same time as Jesus said the same thing: "If you are God, prove it to me." Jesus, God's Son, performed countless miracles while on earth. Why did he do that? The people had heard for years about a Messiah who would come to save them. But knowing something in your head and accepting it in your heart are two entirely different matters. Jesus was God sent to earth to walk, talk, and touch human beings so they would realize with their hearts that he not only existed but longed for a personal relationship with his creation.

But when we try to comprehend God, we often put him in a little box, like John Denver did to "God"—and we say to him (or we think), "If you are God, prove it to me."

- If you are God, fix this mess in my life.
- If you are God, heal my loved one of cancer.
- If you are God, find my child who ran away and bring her home.
- If you are God, get me that promotion at work. I really need the money.
- If you are God, find me a spouse.
- If you are God, change my spouse.

But you see, all of those proofs are focused on the now (the short-term) rather than eternity (the long-term).

What proofs would it take for you to believe that God is God? To grasp the vast nature of who God is and all that he has created, and that no one created him?

Those who didn't understand that in Jesus' day sneered at him as he hung on the cross in agony. "He saved others; let him save himself if he is the Christ of God, the Chosen One."[2]

> *How easy it would have been for Jesus to just lift his pinky finger in their direction . . . and they'd have been ashes.*

The soldiers mocked him too: "If you are the king of the Jews, save yourself."[3]

The discipline Jesus exerted on that cross was unbelievable. He had the awesome power of God, the Creator of the universe, in his fingertips. How easy it would have been for Jesus to just lift his pinky finger in their direction—*zzztttt*—and they'd have been ashes.

I'd have done it if I had that kind of power. You most likely would have too. That's because I know my vindictive, "you'll get yours" side would have come out with a vengeance at such treatment.

But Jesus didn't nuke 'em. All he said was, "Father, forgive them, for they do not know what they are doing."[4] Jesus was focused on the mission—what the Father wanted him to do. And that was far more important than the temporary mocking, the jeering, and even the tremendous physical torment he was going through.

We all know the right thing to do—but we don't do it. We don't finish our missions. We get sidetracked by the events of life, weighed down by the burdens of expectations and the difficult twists on the journey.

Jesus was the perfect one, the sinless one. We human beings are far from perfect. We're going to fail . . . then fail again.

Recently I had a guy tell me, "I understand what you're saying about God being merciful when we fail, but this is the fifth time I've tried to quit smoking, and I failed again. I've given up."

"So?" I said. "I'm fat. I've been on numerous diets. And I've eaten a whole Marie Callender's pie in one sitting. Now what do you want to talk about?"

"I'm fat. I've been on numerous diets. And I've eaten a whole Marie Callender's pie in one sitting."

Too many of us continue to beat ourselves up for our failures. We put God in that little box too. *Well, if he truly is God, then he wouldn't want anything to do with imperfect me.*

Then there are the others of us who have a wee bit too much ego involved—even if we don't realize how cocky we are.

The other day in traffic, I saw a car whose bumper sticker proudly proclaimed, "God is my copilot."

Oh, really? God's your copilot? He's not the pilot? He's "co," or equal, with you?

I don't think so.

If you don't understand who God is, then you can't acknowledge who he is—the almighty Creator of the universe who doesn't need your copiloting help on anything.

> *God's your copilot? He's not the pilot? He's "co," or equal, with you? I don't think so.*

When we understand who God is and we acknowledge who he is, then we can grapple with one of the biggest questions humankind asks: If God is in control, then why do bad things happen? Was he just looking the other way when a young couple and their three children were killed in the middle of an intersection by a drunk driver? Or when your elderly neighbor's house burned to the ground because of faulty wiring?

When God created the universe, he put into play certain physical and spiritual laws. So when a driver drives south in a northbound lane, innocent people are going to pay for that mistake. When the electrician makes a wrong judgment about wiring, the result is that your neighbor loses his house.

God isn't a puppeteer who controls humankind like marionettes on a string. Things happen because the physical and spiritual laws he put into place are violated.

> *God isn't a puppeteer who controls humankind like marionettes on a string.*

Is God all-knowing? Yes.

All-powerful? Yes.

Always present? Yes.

But many of our maladies are a direct result of human free will and choice, which God has allowed. Grist for the mill indeed, isn't it, for all of us who grapple with bad things happening even to good people?

The God we worship is awesome. He can create a daffodil in all its intricacies; he instills the aroma of the hyacinth. His creation is the majestic proof of his power. This same God encircled Tucson, Arizona, with incredibly beautiful mountains. He formed the oceans and all the sea creatures in them. You mean to say that the God who did all this can't help you with the problems you face on a daily basis?

"But Dr. Leman, I'm an insignificant factory worker in Moline, Illinois. Why would God care about me?" you say.

The reality is that God sent his only Son to die on a Roman cross in a very terrible way so that each of us, *if we acknowledge him*, can spend eternity with him in heaven.

Now that's a pretty good deal, factory worker in Moline.

But God is a jealous God. He's not your copilot. You can't put him in a box. He doesn't need to prove anything to you, his creation. And you can't give him your "best shot." He's not interested in your second-best effort of believing in him. With God, it's all or nothing.

Things to Ponder . . .

"In all your ways acknowledge him."

PROVERBS 3:6A

When have you played the "If you are God . . ." game to try to control God? Did it work? Why or why not?

How would acknowledging who God really is help you
grapple with bad things happening to good people?

*To acknowledge God, you
have to act, instead of waiting for
the thunderbolt from the sky.*

10

The Road Less Traveled . . .
Has Fewer People on It

And he will make **your paths** straight.

PROVERBS 3:6B

I've always loved the classic poem by Robert Frost, "The Road Not Taken." It talks about a traveler who stands in the woods, looking at two diverging paths, trying to decide which one to take. Both look good, but he still has to make a decision—a decision that could affect his life in the future.

You might think that such a famous poet as Robert Frost had it made. But his life path was full of surprises—and not all of them happy ones.

Robert Frost was born in San Francisco. His father, a journalist, died when Frost was 11. He was only able to attend a few months of college, and he worked numerous jobs, including at a textile mill and as a teacher, for the next 10 years. He tried sending his poems to the *Atlantic Monthly*, but they were returned with a terse note.

> We regret that *The Atlantic* has no place for your vigorous verse.

That was not a compliment.

Finally Frost sold his farm and took his wife and four young children to England. There he finally published his first collection of poems when he was 39.[1]

It all goes to show that no one's life path is devoid of obstacles; every life has surprises ... even huge curveballs. Like the family whose 15-year-old daughter is now having her seventh surgery. Or the God-honoring man who fell off a golf cart, damaged two areas of his brain, and now struggles to relearn life skills, while his wife works full-time to have income for the family and nearly singlehandedly raises their four young children. Or the woman who gave 20 years of her life to the job she loved, only to be betrayed by a jealous supervisor who stole the credit for all her work and then fired her. Or the father whose wife left him with their two young daughters to go "find herself."

Nobody said life would be easy. But with tenacity and long-term perspective, we can make it through the curves of life and back onto the path. Have no doubt: you *will* fail at some things in life. There's a reason God's grace exists. I, for one, need a lot of it. But when you fail to walk a straight path, don't excuse yourself. Excuses only make the weak weaker. Admitting when and where you strayed is the healthy thing to do and gets your relationships with God and others back on the right track.

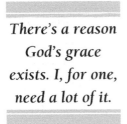

There's a reason God's grace exists. I, for one, need a lot of it.

But let me ask you something. Do you know where you're going in life? Are you aiming, as much as humanly possible, toward your destination? Or are you simply drifting from signpost to signpost along the way, hoping that somehow, somewhere, life might make sense? If you don't know your destination, then you won't even know when you stray off the path.

God doesn't care about your outward success; he cares about your commitment to your faith and the paths he has called you to walk on. Note that Proverbs 3:6 doesn't say *path*; it says *paths*. That means God will call you to walk multiple paths, not only one path. So when your road diverges and you have a choice, as Robert Frost did in "The Road Not Taken," why not think of it as a new opportunity rather than a crisis?

But note that you are responsible for your own path, not for anyone else's. This little snippet of Proverbs has been wrongly used by people who believe that if they merely trust and pray hard enough, they can change others . . . like the woman who told me she was staying in an abusive relationship because she was "trusting God to change that man."

May I be blunt? There are some people and some relationships that cannot be made straight because one of the people in the relationship is not willing to change and is downright sinful. *Sin* is a word not often used in our culture because people are afraid they might make someone feel guilty. Well, some people need a good dose of guilt. And others need to stand up for themselves and hold a wrongdoer accountable.

However, if you're the one who has strayed from the path, there's great news to celebrate. God gives us the ability to get on the right path if we've been on the wrong one. In fact, he longs for us to do so. And he's waiting, with arms outstretched, to welcome us.

It's never too late to step back on the path.

Just ask Robert Frost. He ought to know.

Things to Ponder . . .

"And he will make your paths straight."
PROVERBS 3:6B

Do you believe that there can be more than one "right path" for you to take in life? Why or why not?

How has this book changed your perspective of who God is? Of how he works? Of your relationship with him?

Twists in your life path are not to be feared. They're simply new directions and new opportunities.

A Permanent Record

Write them on the tablet of your heart.

PROVERBS 3:3B

I want to make something completely clear. If heaven ain't fun, I want no part of it. In the book *Heaven* by Randy Alcorn (one of the books that has made a significant impact on my life and thinking), one of the things Randy said that struck me the most was that when you enter heaven, there will be a reception line for you. And the ones you love the most will be in that line.

In case you wonder who'll be making those arrangements, you don't have to worry. The one who knows when a sparrow falls, knows the number of hairs on your head, and orchestrates the entire universe can certainly handle the guest list for you.[1]

I am convinced that everyone is put on this earth for a reason. I used to apologize for using humor everywhere I go. Then, 25 years ago, I realized humor is a gift from Almighty God—a legacy that I can pass on to others. One of my life goals since that time has been to spread joy, to love people, and to help people wherever I go. And I want to do it with all my heart.

> *Everyone is put on this earth for a reason.*

Do you really love God and others with your whole heart? Have you written Proverbs 3:1–6 on the tablet of your heart?

Each of us has an appointment with death someday. Where we go after that is based on what our heart was about.

Were you driven toward helping others because the Spirit of God was alive in you? Did others come to mind before yourself? Or did you focus on yourself and your family to the exclusion of others?

What you do in life matters. It matters to you. It matters to those around you. And it matters to God.

How you live your life now is a legacy for the generations to come. Thinking about that a few times a day certainly would help put life's happenings in perspective, wouldn't it?

Proverbs 3:1–6 promises that if you don't forget God's teachings, you keep his commands in your heart, you trust in him with all your heart, and you acknowledge him in all you do, then you'll receive these things for starters . . . and more:

> *What you do in life matters. It matters to you. It matters to those around you. And it matters to God.*

- a long, fulfilled life
- prosperity
- a good name
- straight paths

That's a powerful prescription for a satisfying, fulfilling life from the way of the wise. It's wisdom with a smile.

I guarantee it.

Notes

Chapter 2: "Jesus and God, Jesus and God, That's All They Talk about—Jesus and God"

1. Matthew 5:39.
2. Psalm 22:1, 16, 18.
3. John 19:24.
4. See Matthew 27:35; Mark 15:24; Luke 23:34; John 19:23–24.
5. Isaiah 53 and Jeremiah 23:5 are a couple examples.
6. Isaiah 53:5.
7. Jeremiah 1:5.

Chapter 3: Jesus Ain't the Big, Bad Wolf

1. Ricks-Bricks, "The Three Little Pigs," http://www.shol.com/agita/pigs.htm, accessed February 10, 2012.

2. Elisabeth Kuhn, "Effects of Stress: Deadly Stress—Seven Ways in Which Too Much Unrelenting Stress Can Kill You," NY Wellness Guide, http://www.nywellnessguide.com/mind/090310-StressEffects.php, accessed March 26, 2011.

3. "Do Positive People Live Longer?" Between Us Boomers, April 18, 2011, http://betweenusboomers.com/do-positive-people-live-longer; "Marital Fidelity Linked to Less Stress, Long, Healthy Life," Malcolmy in News; http://cacheme.wordpress.com/2011/02/14/marital-fidelity-linked-to-less-stress-long-healthy-life/, accessed June 13, 2011.

4. See Matthew 23:27.
5. Romans 7:24.
6. See Romans 8:38–40.
7. Psalm 46:10.
8. Psalm 23:1–3.
9. See John 8:11.
10. Revelation 3:20.
11. See Genesis 5:27.

Chapter 4: Attention, Walmart Shoppers: Jesus Has Left the Building

1. John 9:25.
2. See John 2:1–11.
3. John 2:11.
4. See John 14:1–9.
5. Malachi 3:10.
6. "Quotations for Sweetest Day," The Quote Garden, http://www.quotegarden.com/sweetest-day.html, accessed April 30, 2012.
7. Matthew 25:40.

Chapter 5: I'm All Yours—All 96 Percent!

1. Hebrews 11:1.
2. See Matthew 8:26.
3. See Matthew 28:20 and Acts 1:8.

Chapter 6: The Marines (and God) Need a Few Good Men . . . and Women

1. United States Attorney Southern District of New York, "Bernard L. Madoff Pleads Guilty to Eleven-Count Criminal Information and Is Remanded into Custody," March 12, 2009, http://www.justice.gov/usao/nys/pressreleases/March09/madoffbernardpleapr.pdf.
2. "John Wooden Quotes," Brainy Quote, http://www.brainyquote.com/quotes/authors/j/john_wooden.html, accessed February 10, 2012.
3. "John Wooden Quotes," Brainy Quote, http://www.brainyquote.com/quotes/authors/j/john_wooden_2.html, accessed February 10, 2012.

4. Ibid.

5. Ibid.

6. "John Wooden: Quotes," Goodreads, http://www.goodreads.com/author/quotes/23041.John_Wooden, accessed April 30, 2012.

7. Ibid.

8. Ibid.

Chapter 7: You're the Potter, I'm the Clay . . . But I Do Have a Few Suggestions

1. John H. Sammis, "Trust and Obey," 1887, http://www.cyberhymnal.org/htm/t/r/trstobey.htm.

2. See Romans 7:14–20.

3. Matthew 6:10.

Chapter 8: God Doesn't Want to Be Your #1

1. Romans 14:10–11.

2. Psalm 111:10.

3. Song of Solomon 2:15.

Chapter 9: God Is Not Your Copilot

1. *Oh, God!*, directed by Carl Reiner (Burbank, CA: Warner Bros. Pictures, 1977).

2. Luke 23:35.

3. Luke 23:37.

4. Luke 23:34.

Chapter 10: The Road Less Traveled . . . Has Fewer People on It

1. "Robert Frost Biography," Famous Poets and Poems, http://famouspoetsandpoems.com/poets/robert_frost/biography, accessed May 2, 2011.

A Permanent Record

1. See Matthew 10:29–31.

About
Dr. Kevin Leman

An internationally known psychologist, radio and television personality, and speaker, **Dr. Kevin Leman** has taught and entertained audiences worldwide with his wit and commonsense psychology.

The *New York Times* bestselling and award-winning author of *Have a New Kid by Friday, Have a New Husband by Friday, Have a New You by Friday, Sheet Music*, and *The Birth Order Book* has made thousands of house calls for radio and television programs, including *Fox & Friends, The View*, Bill Bennett's *Morning in America*, Fox's *The Morning Show, Today, The 700 Club, Oprah*, CBS's *The Early Show, In the Market with Janet Parshall*,

Live with Regis Philbin, CNN's *American Morning*, *Life Today* with James Robison, and *Focus on the Family*. Dr. Leman has also served as a contributing family psychologist to *Good Morning America*.

Dr. Leman is the founder and president of Couples of Promise, an organization designed and committed to help couples remain happily married. His professional affiliations include the American Psychological Association, the American Federation of Television and Radio Artists, and the North American Society of Adlerian Psychology.

In 2003, the University of Arizona awarded Dr. Leman the highest award they can give to one of their own: the Distinguished Alumnus Award. In 2010, North Park University awarded him an honorary Doctor of Humane Letters degree.

Dr. Leman received his bachelor's degree in psychology from the University of Arizona, where he later earned his master's and doctorate degrees. Originally from Williamsville, New York, he and his wife, Sande, live in Tucson, Arizona. They have five children and two grandchildren.

For information regarding speaking availability, business consultations, seminars, or the annual Couples of Promise cruise, please contact:

Dr. Kevin Leman
P.O. Box 35370
Tucson, Arizona 85740
Phone: (520) 797-3830
Fax: (520) 797-3809
www.birthorderguy.com
www.drleman.com

Resources by Dr. Kevin Leman

Books for Adults

Have a New Kid by Friday

Have a New Husband by Friday

Have a New Teenager by Friday

Have a New You by Friday

The Birth Order Book

The Way of the Wise

What a Difference a Mom Makes

What a Difference a Daddy Makes

Under the Sheets

Sheet Music

Making Children Mind without Losing Yours

It's a Kid, Not a Gerbil!

Born to Win

Sex Begins in the Kitchen

7 Things He'll Never Tell You . . . But You Need to Know

What Your Childhood Memories Say about You

Running the Rapids

The Way of the Shepherd (written with William Pentak)

Becoming the Parent God Wants You to Be

Becoming a Couple of Promise

A Chicken's Guide to Talking Turkey with Your Kids about Sex (written with Kathy Flores Bell)

First-Time Mom

Step-parenting 101

Living in a Stepfamily without Getting Stepped On

The Perfect Match

Be Your Own Shrink

Stopping Stress before It Stops You

Single Parenting That Works

Why Your Best Is Good Enough

Smart Women Know When to Say No

Books for Children, with Kevin Leman II

My Firstborn, There's No One Like You

My Middle Child, There's No One Like You

My Youngest, There's No One Like You

My Only Child, There's No One Like You

My Adopted Child, There's No One Like You

My Grandchild, There's No One Like You

DVD/Video Series for Group Use

Have a New Kid by Friday

Making Children Mind without Losing Yours
(Christian—parenting edition)

Making Children Mind without Losing Yours
(Mainstream—public school teacher edition)

Value-Packed Parenting

Making the Most of Marriage

Running the Rapids

Single Parenting That Works

Bringing Peace and Harmony to the Blended
Family

DVDs for Home Use

Straight Talk on Parenting

Why You Are the Way You Are

Have a New Husband by Friday

Have a New You by Friday

Available at 1-800-770-3830 or www.drleman.com or www.birthorderguy.com

Visit DrLeman.com
for more information, resources, and videos from his popular books.

Follow Dr. Kevin Leman on

 Dr Kevin Leman

 drleman

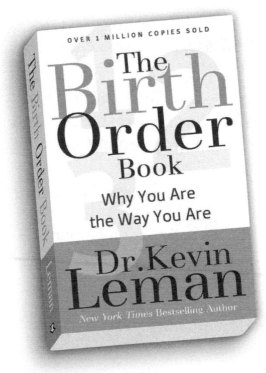

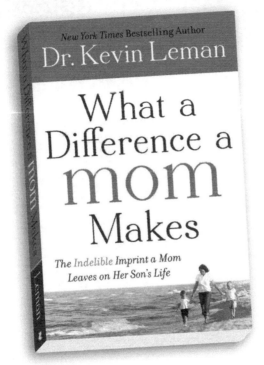

Kid-tested,
parent-approved

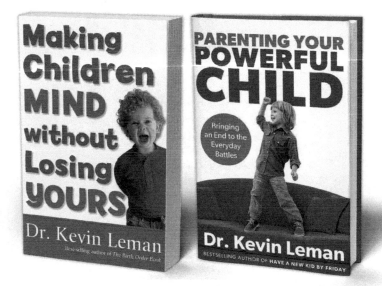

If anyone understands why children behave the way they do, it's Dr. Kevin Leman. Let him teach you a loving, no-nonsense parenting approach that really works.